# songs for leaving
## a.s. coomer

# gutter snob books

# Songs for Leaving

Editor: Michele McDannold

Gutter Snob Books
200 W. Main St., #209
Trinidad, CO  81082

For Louis

# Contents

# songs for leaving

## Shipwrecked on Liminal Island

I.

It tastes of darkness
An inky black blurring blue

The pills leave you spinning
A birch leaf perched on the surface
The waters turbulent, rising all around

Observe the new confluences
Know you're in a reprieve
An island for now

It is trauma that can't be stolen
Scars picked for fresh blood
Momentary purpled continents

Dry for now

II.

It fills your body
A claustrophobic red stretch
Frightener fingers prod and squeeze
There're no seams, just a rending

The fabric old & only getting older
Frayed like tarp, flayed like carp
Arrayed with a tired, well-trod fascination

Obsessed for now

III.

Sift through the sieve
See just how permeable

Grasp at the passing stream
Hold onto the nothing that surrounds you

IV.

Pick up pen, dirty paper
Wean poison from fang
Stir it into strong black coffee

Greet the day
Know it will exact its revenge
For crimes you didn't even know you committed
But feel guilty for now

The future a fence for your memories & misunderstandings

The horizon a dislocated jaw of burning houses
Glinting like tombstones in the sun

Look for your place while covering your tracks
Most endings are other stories' beginnings
& nobody likes a spoiler

& everybody likes a surprise

V.

Search for the thread
Without compromising your direction
Know it all crosses somewhere,

Sometime down the line

Consult your watch
Consult your holy words
Consult your bank account

If you've still got teeth
Gnash, grind it down
Until you can choke it down

Consult your childhood memories
Consult your precognitions
Consult your dreams

If you're thrown from the train
Take comfort
It's just a trip of a different sort

Consult your doctor
Consult your pharmacist
Consult the first responders

Live in the expanding space between words
Too much to say but so little will to speak
Understand something will always be lost
         In translation

VI.

Know it will have its way

Hum along to that Narcan spiritual
         An unexpected crossover hit
Dunked in darkness
Baptized in it

Pulled wide-eyed & terrified
Back into the world of the living

Hoarse even in silence,
Screaming a thousand choruses
To the same tired song

*I-didn't-want-to-be-here*s melding with
    *It-hurts-too-much*
*Enough-is-never-enough*s harmonizing with
    *I-can't-help-it*
Everything rhyming with
    *The Big Game Is Every Night*

VII.

It gives more than just a taste

Mute with filters
Trim like prints
Wear shadow shrouds

Hide the mental limp
With unimportances
Distractionizations
*Lie*-lies

Fall into the pall

VIII.

Know it will have its way

IX.

Despite *it*,
Despite it *all*:
Make, do, see

If you're able:
Do, see, make

If you can now:
See, make, do

Everybody:
Do, make, see

X.

Afterclap
Full dark

**existential motion sickness, a highway lullaby**

me & my bullshit
hit the road
bright & early
when i think
i'm at my best

me behind the wheel
sipping chicory coffee
from a stained thermos
eyes peeled for the 5-0
right hand at 2 wrenching
      like grinding teeth
      each knuckle jawsore
      periodically popping
      like muted snares
left hand scooping arcs of
humid time from the open window
      catching waves
      fluttering to return
      dancing like ghosts
      in the late May breeze

bs shouts directions
over overblown factory speakers
      some indecipherable
      nirvana b-side
trying to outroar the wind rushing
off another shining eighteen-wheeler
shedding truck wash tears
in crystalline splashes
on our bugpocked windshield

we're forty-nine miles out

he's said three times already
    just another
    in a long succession
    of lies and/or mistakes
hang a richard, he says
    false surety puffing
    his florid cheeks
this after three louises
    back-to-back-to-back

i don't say nothing
    hardly do these days
    guess my tombstone'll
    be another's sad refrain

## don't try

    hey bluebird
    looking at you
    maybe we'll sing
    that song together
    some blue evening

i wonder how many wrongs
    make a right
    how far down this road
    will we take it?
    will we make it?

i signal the turn
like every turn
i've ever taken

bs smirks as i check
then recheck the mirrors
for accidents lurking

in my blind spots

bs asking me what for
there's somebody there
or there ain't
what's another day anyway?

if free will is the proverbial free meal
we'd never need to signal a turn

i wonder out loud
if comas are restful

bs: that was yer turn

we watch it go by
coasting ten miles
over the posted speed

me: shit, but it didn't look like the highway

bs: we got a few more
of these here
backroads
before then

how many times
have we sang
that song?

susurrated static snow
from a long fadeout
        another studio session
        that got way out of hand

the song ends
as i turn into
an empty driveway
        another burnt-out
        single wide
        mobile mausoleum
        blanketed by kudzu
trying to turn around
        ain't i always
        trying to turn
        it all around?

bs breathes so heavy
it's nearly a pant
he alternates between
sucking in whistling air
through flaring nostrils
& gulping through
gaping graveyard mouth

i'm never sure if he's putting me on
but I can tell he's struggling too
we carry each other's burdens
the way lovers often do
every so often
he even
chips in
on gas

i crank up the volume
put the car back in D
knowing with a blossoming
understanding that we'll never
        get     there
that there was never anywhere

to       get to
&, really, why can't we take
a sunday drive on any
ol' day we choose?

what is time
but another
interstate
backing up
with no exit
in sight

## Lost Your Keys

*It was not Death, for I stood up,*
*And all the Dead, lie down—*
        Emily Dickinson

Heavy be these feet
Though they haven't shuffled
Their distinctive skit-drag
Oversized moccasin slapback boogie

Weary be these thoughts
Narrow paths trod-worn
Nosebleed running
Branching farther at each fork
Crisscrossing the rolling hills of your mind
Like William Tecumseh Sherman with his wake
Making small anything capable
Of one day becoming large

Empty be these memory cells
The jailer lost his keys
You're the jailer, lost your keys
Have you traded your Never-Forgets
For complete immersion in The Present?
This beam of slanted afternoon sunlight
For entire pages of your mental scrapbook?

Receding stygian tide kept barely at bay
White-cap wolf's fangs
Shattering on the other side of the breakers
A proximity reminder
You're never very far from the drop-off
And, oh yes, the waters will rise again
That Hangdog Moon will find

The Hair of the Dog that Bit Us All
& come back to drown & flood

Frozen be these actions
Arrested by indecision
Each choice a shackle of another sort
Directions & their corresponding dominos
Made from your bird bones, clacking
To the rhythm of a song just outside
Your range of hearing & comprehension
Sound colors you cannot see
Shades of grey in a colorless panoply
What little Dignity there was is squandered
Sold like a yard sale quilt for pocket lint

Ringing like tinnitus and the wind
Taking something more
Than was bargained for
Hand still sore from the sudden handshake
The unasked for Gift of Life
& the body's rugged determination
To persevere at all costs
Clasp & release, but long is the embrace

It wasn't Death, the dead don't dance
It was her kissing cousin
Scythe swinging like pendulous breasts
Swooping low to aim high
Cloaked hip sashaying to the rhythm
Of yet another World-Ender's pastiche triptych
Another Psalmist's hymn of devastation
An echo of an echo of a Rending

On tremulous legs
I stood on quaking ground

Unsure, but standing just the same
Alive & ashamed but keeping time
Despite these two hoofed left feet

**Songs for Leaving (A Spider's Lyre & A Liar's Yarn)**

I.

Home is knowing
It can't rain forever

  Sing it three times
  Please let it be so

Four wicks encased
Pirouettes in cracked glass
Red-eyed & mesmerized

Dragging my hairy tongue down
Oil-slickened cobblestoned alleys
Asking every ghost I meet
The way to Fascination Street

II.

Great pale circadian shuffle
Dance the ¡Perceived Indignation!
To the mournful soul's didgeridoo solo
  Shake it, Wallflower

Swaying familiar rhythms
Cascading three-part harmonies
Clucking banjo & mando pick tinkles
Everyone shit-kick strutting
Believing life ain't half as bad
As it could've been

III.

The tape warbles
Giving what can be
Such a cold song warmth

For a while there
Our song leaked
Spilling too much
Of what we have
        So little of

But the current
Only goes the one way
& I figure we'll pick it back up

It's just turtles all the way down after all

IV.

Runoff susurration
Silted conversation

Glinting moans of flint
Whisper-singing radiant psalms

We start the day in fog
We end the night in smoke

        Sing it three times
        Please let it be so

V.

Wipe earned sweat
With sun-warmed palm
        A mini-timpani splash

Hear the sound
Of one-hundred breaking levees
Look down
At hands on steel-bodied guitar
        —A spider's lyre & a liar's yarn

Little repetitions
Variations on a theme
Another river
Jumping        banks

New meanings bent    from rigidity's confines
Ethos meandering    hunter green like the Nolin

The old molded
Through experience
Kneaded like dough
Under the cosmic baker's floury knuckles
Eroding psychic cancer
        As the years stack up
        —Lean, Babel, lean—
        We wean what we need
        Damn the rest
Wisdom radiation

VI.

Songs for life
Songs for learning

& later
Songs for leaving

You know the words

We light the new day's fire
With yesterday's glowing embers

Sing it three times
Please let it be so

### Droste Effect Armageddon with Infinite Recursions

I.

I'm a liar
Been spinning yarns
Since I was a snotnose
Little lies

## Big ones too

The kind that trip you up
The kind that keep you
From falling down
&, especially, the kind that make for a good story

Never let the truth
Get in the way of a good story

II.

Each a brick or plank
A hallway leading nowhere
A staircase to solid ceiling
My life the Winchester Mystery House

In the heyday of endless construction
Workers busy with they knew not what
The plans secret, no one surprised
To find no guiding hand at the wheel

A sleepwalker's design
Architectural astral projection
The house not a home
But a lie within a lie

Nesting dolls in a babushka abode
Purpose obscured, made ornamental

Some lies are told for the telling

III.

I'm not good with the truth
        —Who is these days?
There are things we tell ourselves
        Patently untrue
That keep the wheels turning
The truth an impurity, bad gas
Gumming up the works

Or a wrench in the churning cogs
All that metal-on-metal screaming
Sparking like shrapnel on ornate armor
Coming to rest in the silence of sudden stillness

Allow no time for cogitation
Regurgitate untruths
Stack 'em up for the liar's pyre
A vain bonfire of inanities

Snapped kindling ready to burn
Next lie a scratched match
Fiery head of sashaying flame
High-stepping towards spreading accelerant

IV.

We're all burning down
The house that truth built

Some accidentally
Greasy hullaballoos
Made worse by the tossing of water
       Watch the wallpaper curl

Breathe in the billowing smoke
Understand there is no way out

Then there're the nihilistic arsonists
Harebrained immolators with itchy fingers

Circling coyotes cackling like hyenas
       A predator's kaleidoscopic rotation
       Electric fangs rending neon flesh
Bleeding flashes over another combustible wound

V.

Lies like ice under fresh fluffy powder
Lies like splintered glass in the grass
       —Have fun digging out the shards

Roll & tumble lies
Rough & rowdy lies
Yard sale lies
Wholesale lies
Discount lies
Outlaw living lies
Blue period blue lies

Bureaucratic red tape lies
Oil-drenched American Dream lies
Changing of the guard lies
       Another velvet cloaked coup
       Hordes of handless crooks with nothing to do

Lies as lowdown as the Mariana Trench
Everest high lies, avalanche lies
  Bellowing down the mountain with a banjo on
its knee
  Stripped poplar neck with catgut strings
  Singing just to see what each lie brings

Desert fox with pink rattlesnake in mouth lies
Owl cutting the whip-poor-will's song short lies

Pounding only the black keys lies
Moon-dipped sonata lies, morning ray aubade lies

  & all the little white ones too

VI.

Crushed under the weight of a great collective lie
Black hole gravity lies filling our pneumonic lungs

Collapses on top of collapses
A calamitous ouroboros

Droste effect Armageddon with infinite recursions

VII.

Fill the swan's marrow with lead
  & see how far we make it across the pond

## Riversong (Memorial Potamology)

As we lay low
Another of the gifted

A stray feather flutter-step dancing
Above the shifting snowpack

Drifts down to join the snowmelt
Another drop in the flow

Downstream, the dream everchanging
You'll never wade out into the same river

No one ever does
Life a timelapse of the flood

We count the hours by the silt rings
Left on the sodden warping walls

With each tick a lessening
Recession gradual but never quite complete

Nature's song swells
We bleed as we sing

❋

Those left behind
Met at the haunt

A flotilla of ghostships
Circling a single, tired mooring

We offered up our songs

Words swirling skyward in cloudsmoke

Raining down on brittle snowcrust
Easing towards a lessening

Erosion, sure, but welcome
Against choking alluvium

Our vice hardened hearts clotting
With detritus, mangled branches

& shorn shingles, mistakes & reckonings,
Otters, coots, and mallards displaced

Rain-soaked refugees wading
Through muck and debris

Seeking new, higher banks
Just like the rest of us

&ast;

There are those that take advantage
Use the roiling for dumping off

Tires and garbage, old appliances
& the lapped smooth stones of need

You can find them on the bridges
Shifty eyes scanning for witnesses

Dropping what is bald and useless
End over end ending in a splash wave

Lost in the tumultuous brown churning

The waters accept with indifference

Burying under or carrying along
Another abandoned verse of riversong

## Singing Sour Grapes

When hope feels like the kink in the hose
'cos what isn't a garden after all?
& the dilapidated walls of your heart
Black and gettin' blacker
Give up the ghost & all things corporeal
Sagging, all of it sagging
Flow below the valley low
The muddy water, grit in the teeth, stingers in the eyes
Will be the least of the molehills-turned-mountains
The range arranged in a range in a rage
You're able to appreciate as your problems

Grapes unfit for anyone's table wine
& whine you must but rust crusts the busted backseat springs
& there ain't no room left upfront

Behind the black patch
Cracked blinds & misplaced time
Great heaping sweeps as deep as the dreams of The Last Sleep
You're given the fence and a running start
But find the sheep stygian & immune to "how high?"
Pinky promises of "gettin' by, by & large" in the cloven-footed
future
A goat's head soup of potential failures
Hoping against hope the sweet by-&-by's more than this pigsty
Just another place in time to whither, rot, & die slowly
& just long enough for a Lot's-Wife of a Last Look
At the breadcrumb trail of tiny failures
Each glistening under the midnight sun
Glinting like broken geodes
Or splintered glass
An eternal exhale of indecision

**Where Can We Grow If Not the Garden? (Invasive Blues)**

Desire twines, honeysuckle chokes
       Coiled cords climb
       Over flower & vegetable
       All these seeds we slipped
            Into our toiled soil
            Lovingly tended to
               & watered
       Smothered into a pale withered mess

Chinese wisteria vines over
       Cucumbers & raspberries
       You & your still water
       & me with my sweet tooth

Ache like bulb near bloom
       Like hungry hummingbird
       Like root-gnawn iris
       Like back after weeding
       Like sleep-deprived mind
       Like every minute of every night

    ✺

Hollowed out by a deeper need
       Lit up with jack-o'-lantern flickers
       Shadows darkened by the danse of flame
            In the touch of lips
            By moonlit whispers
            Of another lover's name

There's rot in vulnerability
But silent resentment creeps

Up the bamboo trellises
Meant for our seedling hearts
& we just can't have that,
            Now, can we?

Fantasy like mint in the garden
            Wildfire spread
            Rejection dread
            Upturned cloud-kissing
            Mammoth sunflower heads
            Honeybee honey
            Glaze on honeydew
            Honey locust bristles
            & cedar sap dripping
                        Down bark
                        & stem
                        Gumming up
                                    While slowly
                                                Falling down

Longing like kudzu suffocating
            Rolling hills
            Abandoned coal mines
            Slumped tobacco barns
            & every door left open
                        A touch too long


            ✳

Purple loosestrife & blue-black tribulations
Weathered with more than a touch of poison

A late frost took the first sown
Beetles & worms
            Every shoot's seventh son

Until Sevin dust blankets
     Like snow

     Here
Mind-to & begging
Libido & deprivation
Common joy & ordinary suffering

     & there
Quackgrass & briars
Canada thistle & ragweed
Russian sage & shoots of wild onion
Sprout before the broken vessels
     Of our tired, swollen eyes

There's nothing for it
But to weed 'em when you see 'em
     Sink fingertips into churned earth
     Seek thickening root neck & squeeze

Keep singing that invasive plaint
'til you convince yourself
     "This ain't no
     Hard row to hoe.
     Lord, no,
     This ain't no
     Hard row to hoe."

## Gundrunk Blues
*for Uvalde*

Bullets pump from the chambers of our magnum hearts
Lead and cordite course through our clotted veins
Poisoned blood singing songs of annihilation
       Psalms of death

Our love on sale in the gun case
Thoughts & prayers scribbled illegibly on the receipt
       All sales final, no returns

We told our children we'd do better
That this would never happen again
Not to us      but here we are
Toeing the line
Nearing the cliff
      Falling

Is there no bottom?

Hear the spent rounds
Clink against each other
      Ceaselessly tolling death knells
      Never-ending
Hear the classroom doors locking
      In vain
Hear the school chairs thrown away
      From the knee-high tables
Panting fear huddled underneath
      Shaking
          Crying
              Helpless

Feel the impact before you hear the blast

When will the body count be high enough?
      Isn't one too many?
How much money will it take to save our children?
When will *our* politicians stop voting with *their* wallets?
How many more verses of this godawful song must we
sing?

✳

Uvalde's song slips into the stygian stream
Quit your rowing, jettison the oars
Give up bailing the rising water
It's useless if we let this divide chasm
If we don't stop the darkness
      From flooding in
We're all going down with this ship

## night looms blues

### I.

passages barred
narrowed like slaughterhouse chutes
pinpoint paranoia bleeds
staining & paralyzing into indecision
an anxious buddha whispering
    *don't try*
over & over again
fretfully inactive

### II.

stacking seconds like kindling
feeding daytime flames
    begrudging their dance
    trying not to stare
hoping there'll be enough
left over for the glacial night ahead

### III.

behind a smear of muted specifics
generalizations masquerade as memory
stories as scents carried off in a stiff wind
recounted versions smell right but taste off
    saccharine or so bitter they're sweet
    depending on the company
        a bastard love in the fury
        a keening love swirling below
my recollections collect little embellishments
twisted twines coat and vine
& the truth, this time,

is a near rhyme

IV.

failure expectation as pre-storm news coverage
the endless waiting broken
by a shot of the ocean receding
before the big wave
          knowing another's on the way
crushing the sand between my toes
          each grain a cringe, a tear,
                    a glinting, crystalline fear
          a blurred shot from a clear lens
          going fractal as the pattern repeats
staring at the horizon so long
i'm nothing short of thankful
when it finally whitecaps
          eclipsing the coruscate sun
& finally comes crashing down

# A Medley of Discursive Melodies

Me, the flea
In a panoply
Of need

See me
Slip through
The sieve
Bob & weave
Cling like
The last pleading
Leaf on the tree

We sing
As we flee

Bleeding songs
Golden psalms

Slender, long
Necks kissing
Plying palms

Whispering dreams
Creep into reality
Neon sheen
Dripping with sleaze

Carried off shrieking
On the winged breeze

Let it go

＊

Coming to be
Thee to me
I to we

Hear the whip-
Poor-will sing
Honey to bees
Coming to mean
A little more
Than it seems

See them dance
On the graves
Of these
Sleeping beasts
So beautiful
In their slumber
—& what righteous flashes

In closed-casket-death
Lives open for plunder
Shiny, plastic tulips
Forever in bloom
Under the relentless kisses
Of the fluorescent sun

＊

Sailing missives
Floating frog

Green scum &

Worn words rocking

Shadows          on water
Ripples          in fog
More haze        than smog
*chokingjustthesame*

The owl cries early
Singing out     homing in

The moths beat themselves
To death every night
Their crispy corpses
Pockmark the bottom
Of the spiderwebbed crystal
Where they dust
Under flickering luminosity
          Granulated erosion
          Corrosion to carbon
Waiting on a dutiful tenet
Or at least someone kind
Enough to open a window

※

Train comes round
Straightest stretch
For three & a half counties

Rain slinks down
Embarrassed at all our bodies

          That hangdog moon swoons
          Watches nursing a sweating
                Hair of the dog

While you sit stoned as a log
Rotted all along, embedded
In a putrid perennial miasma

Pain continues to lurk
     Panned like tinnitus
Crossing another border
Fighting the Big Berserk
Hot blue feeling like a jukebox jerk
& you blurt the first five words
That smolder up from the ruins of your brain
& here it is again, the pitter-patter
           of pain
               pain
                 pain

## all graves are dug by the living

*Most of us forgive because we have trespassed not because
we are magnanimous.*
        —Nikki Giovanni, *The Women Gather*

Goddamn is it hard to be kind
When you're dying inside
Kneejerk lashing out
Blaming victims
For perceived weaknesses
Thinking yourself nobler
For your silent but sloppy suffering
Pulling the tablecloth off with you
As you drunkenly fall out of your chair
Ruining everybody's dinner

In the scintillating hangdog morning
You hear of your misdeeds
Head between knees
Bobbing in an unseen stream
You pick at the used gum
In your hair
Try to brush the caked vomit
From your collar
Do your best to ignore everyone's
Purposeful avoidance
Of looking in your direction

You feel simultaneously like you won
& were thwarted some great prize

You tried to control the situation
Until you realized you couldn't
Instead of coming to grips

With the humbling vastness
Of The Big Bad Nothing
& your speck space therein
You snarled a sneer, fulminated
Picked up blind hatred
Like an earworm chorus
& wore it like a new hat
Out into the sunless night

You thought you sent it all spiraling out of control
Thinking chaos poured on chaos
Would put out your own pyre
Serve as a firebreak in the burning valley
Of your drought-stricken heart
But some holes are made without shovels
Most mouths come with feet already inside
& all graves are dug by the living
~~For those already dying~~
~~We're all dying~~

The table is remade
It is tiramisu to decry
Creamed coffee to denounce
Empathy the bleached, reused filter
At the center of it all
Sodden, spent, ready for the compost
The brew is bitter
& sits like castoff oil
In the sour wastes of your hangover belly
Boiling up with the bile
& other waste hate/fear produces
You swallow it back down
Grinding the clinging, chunkier bits
Between your misfiring piston jaws
Until you can attempt to stomach them

Down again
In your sickness
Seeing others eat revolts you
This despite your sweet tooth
This despite your roiling, emptied stomach
This despite everyone's gnawing hunger
You can't stand others enjoying their deserts
So you throw yours against the dining room wall
To watch the whip cream clump
On the shards of someone else's fine China

## Tangled Tape & Fractured Lifelines: the Big Bad Nothin's Reprise

We feign calm
As the televised sky
Screams the screech of bombs

We hiss psalms through gritted teeth
Sweat of supplication
Lining the fractured lifelines of our palms

Static explosions
Fueled by nowhere politics
Killings & imaginary lines
Border lords & refugees
Everybody needing more
Than what's left

They used to beat
Drums in battle
Now heads bow
To the intercontinental
      Ballistic gospel
To the dronesong
      Pushbutton calamities
      On video game screens
To the Big, Bad Nothin'
      Cooing to us all
      An anthem for The Fall
      The know-betters plead
      For deathbed absolution
      But nobody's there
      To answer the call
To the entrenched schisms
      Another broken levee

Offering no protection at all
Spilling in the darkness
Tsunami pall, cresting gall
Cough-spit-choking
But in time at the right times

Arthritic fingers rusty wrench reaching
Stripped bolts & a cracked head gasket
Another lemon engine
  Breaking down
  On the long haul
Another hefty short-term outlay
  Chunking out
  The perpetual
  Overdraw

Thoughts & prayers
Peel back each empathetic layer
Pull the tangled tape from the player
Speak sandbelt, think conveyer

Drown on shore leave, drunken sailor
Empty your heart like the drunk tank
    Of a sleeping jailor
Lift in tornado teeth like a single-wide trailer
& tongue the tired chorus' sugar substitute
  Cotton-mouthed cedar sap sticky think
  Grainy with trash juice aftertaste

Wish for anything but this split-world friction
  That grinds out grout until tiles fall
  That guts insulation and pummels drywall
  That crackles like dancing livewires
    In these ribcage halls

Stand back to see nothing
But the naked bowing studs & collapsing joists
The only thing new a hoary hairy sinkhole opening
Masticated foundation crumbles dropping down
       From the gaping maw
       & gnashing jaws
       Into the relative obscurity
       Of pushpin split-ends
       The unruly follicles
       Of the cosmic beard
       Oiled with radiation

Here come the End Times
       The End Times
           Here come
               The End Times
               fa la lala la

## Another Song of Erosion

I.

There are no whip-poor-wills in the desert
The birds here skitter through brush & arroyo
Light on all the things left abandoned
Sun washed washtubs & bullet riddled stoves
Everything broken & rusted & beautiful
They leave little puffs of dust & the crackle of
Their music races up the pale valley of my back
To nest in the empty space between my ringing, sun-
burnt ears

II.

As we pass under oxidized barbed
Wire clinging to slanted fence posts
I hear the ghosts of rifle reports popping tin cans

I flinch & stutter, trip up but avoid falling down
Watch the orange flakes flit & dance & disappear
Into the sand & stone & glinting glass

In the distance, someone is shooting, a flurry of noise
Followed immediately by another stillness interrupted
This hiss of dust whispering, bedrock exposed & licked
clean

A slow dance of friction & scraping feet
Another song of erosion

III.

We dropped the bomb out here

Another bellowed verse of mankind's siren song

*"I am become death, the destroyer of worlds"*

We carried the mutating rock to the top of the mountain
Swatted sweat from our stinging eyes
Looked down on where we came from
Consulted the clock of mutual destruction
Decided the time was right
Then let it roll back towards the city
So we could watch & shake & see

## The Last Lament, a B-Side Elegy

*It's not dark yet, but it's gettin' there.*
—Bob Dylan

The fall never hurts
It's always the landing

In fact, there's a bastard joy
      In plummeting

Wrapped in gravity's enveloping arms
Pulled into her bosom
      Just as fast
      As you can drop

There, like a wayward bolt of lightning
      A cessation, a letting go
      Ascension in descent
          Reprieve's reprise
          From the squeeze

But you can only fall for so long
Then it's "so long, it's been good to know yuh'"

or a death, yes, but one too long in coming

I can't be the only one
Paralyzed by breathless indecision

I can't be the only one singing these dirges
      Deep cut threnodies
      From The End Time Hymnal
      Bodies sway with palms raised
          Is this supplication or surrender?

Waving or drowning?

No, this can't be The Last Lament
  There're too many
  Songs left to wail
  New interpretations
  To gust battered sails
  Old ways to fail anew

This can't be *Then*
But, Lord, Sweet God
Does it feel like it

*quote from Woody Guthrie's "So Long, It's Been Good
to Know Yuh (Dusty Old Dust)"

## The Slow Dance of Attrition (Waltzing Into Oblivion)

I.

Try looking forward
To a time when you can
Look forward to anything

Keep that nugget of hope
        That shithouse glimmer
In the compost of your chest
Let its rot serve the forest floor
Let its fragrance perfume
The bittersweet ache
        Of summer nights

If there's light
Let it nourish
What soil
We have left
Let it bring the rains
        But not the floods
Let it succor, let it soak

II.

Fight that thief erosion as best you can

My dad built walls along the Nolin
        Cinderblocks and rebar
                Along bank and root

I stacked word on word
        Until I had ducts and pools
                Lived with the spring

Trickling at my feet
Until I had these steep-walled drainage ditches
Everything either swept up & carried away
Or buried under crumbling concrete
Lives pressed together
Like the lavender nestled
In the binding
Of that book of poems
You can't help returning to


We both know we can only win
The everyday battles of our lives
That's the best you can hope for
This war, like most wars, is one-sided
Up until the point it isn't
Sometimes there's a decisive blow
An opportunistic jab landing home
The unexpected haymaker
An answered prayer of desperation
But more often than not it's just that slow dance of
attrition
A two-step shuffle for the end of the world
See me waltzing into oblivion


III.


The great lapping water ripples with moonquake
Unpredicted tides rush & pull
Pulling free what's been hanging loose
What hasn't been tied down is lost
In the churning clusterfuck
The memories of before flicker
Another No Vacancy light
In need of fresh bulbs
& new wiring

These, too, wear away
Until they're placeholder words
Marking moments carried off
In the flashflood of living
    Torrents jumping banks
    Rushing over, burying under
        Here today, gone tomorrow
    Broken oar life raft circling round & round
    The motor fried, useless
        Leaking oily sorrow
        To rainbow slick the surface
        Of the reflected red sun morning

## early summer georgia van gogh

the obgyn
dreams of
birds
fluttering
from the
womb

in her
retelling
i see
the motion
of georgia
o'keeffe's
palate but
vinny van
gogh's
broad
stroked
birds

it ends
with a
gaping
mouth
look up
at the
patient's
open trunk
the uterus
gone

again
o'keeffe

this time
blue &
green music
throbbing
in signac time
with her
rising pulse

strings screech
rise like waves
splashing cacophony
stealing her breath

she wakes
to a renoir smear
that melds into
a blue-black
bedroom cézanne
as the tears clear
& sleep flees
tail tucked
between its
arthritic knees
to hobble out
a drunk bastard's
rocking dance
under the sickly
sickle moon
& pinprick stars

## Just Another October Poem

As the years pass
Piled like deadfall
It seems like more and more
Leaves are cleaved
From these skeletal trees

You'd think they'd stand
Straighter for the loss
But their boughs bow low
Hunched over as if against
Coming winter's wicked-eyed wind

As if the bad things can be avoided
With a simple crouching down

But even the blue moon shines here
You can't live small enough to escape all light

There're shadows, sure,
But they're shallow
Pools not even ankle-deep
Offering nowhere to hide

     Square to circle
Just another place
     Triangle to rectangle
Where you don't fit

And you sit & count the hours
Mouth their names
    3:33, 11:11
Prop up the soldiers that make up the platoon
    1,440 standing at attention

Arrayed in an elaborate formation of surrender
Not enough for that, not enough for this
Until you have a clock of wastefulness

Talks of making the time
Like it's just another daytime television casserole
Comprised of ingredients most pantries keep
Cheese & compromise, noodle & loneliness
The sweet ketchup sauce salted with tears
Gritty with burnt brown sugar

You open the notebook
Smear a little blood on the page
Unsurprised to find clots clinging
To the dispatches of before
Some macabre marginalia
Of the inescapable     slow burn

The kind of fire you can't put out

The old, gnarly oak stump soaked in diesel
& left to smoke under that chickenshit sun

## Wash Stop

I thought you a rainshadow, Holy Faith,
        but you showed me otherwise
Under thunder & spitting rain,
        brick & stone trace a line for the floods
Another hopeful folly but useful
        against the erosion of our lives

        Softer than expected,
I could choke on you—it wouldn't take much
We can dance on chipped bits of lost pottery,
        fling mica-flecked pebbles to skitter & plop
Temporarily halt the rising water
        in the dammed arid
        wastes of our minds

Knowing these petty fortifications will crumble,
        setting silt free
        followed closely by the licking,
the lapping, the great swallowing
up of everything that has ever
        fallen down

## Some Chorus of Impermanence

When I see mountains
I think of impermanence
How even crags crumble

What good are these words?
Inky black splotches
On the backs of cleaved trees
      Pulp, all of it

These snaggle toothed snarls
Of life & love & loss

Not to mention
      beauty

But then there's the glide of the pen
A nearly silent singing
Reverberating echoes of some chorus
Picked up & plucked
From a cobwebbed corner
Of the gray space
You try to ignore

& you find you already know the words
      Ineffable as smoke
      Liminal as running water
& you can't help but sing along

To hell with eternity
I, too, am a rock
A soft one, a minor one
But a part of the mountain
      After all

## Booksong

### I.

Hands: Seismic
In attempt to still
I pick up a book
Throw myself in
Outrun that hungry tide
For a little while
It's a race I know I'll lose
Besides this is executioner weather
Red sun morning, halberds come a-fallin'
All the children singing,
"Fall down on your knees
& pray to the guillotine"

What am I punishing myself for?

### II.

Hot natured
I trace a bead of sweat
Back to its place of origin
A speck where the ridged Sierra Nevada
Of the bridge of your nose
Meets the raked Great Salt Lake
Between your eyebrows where I place
My torn and chapped lips
Reflex devotion
I've always been a man of ritual
Even if faithless
& I won't lie
There was a time
When each raindrop was choreographed

The splashing: divine
Now each ping just upsets still water

I don't know what this says about me
Who knows? Some of it might be true

III.

I wonder if that bit of you loves me
Or if it's only a fairy tale I tuck myself in with
After a while I bet it does & there's the gut punch
The responsibility of such love
The mammoth weight of it
But I've always been a beast of troublesome burden
Condemned Sisyphus slumped but moving,
Whistling back down the mountain
Another hangdog reprisal's reprise
A deepening sweetness ringing like a cavity

There's a part of me always singing
Beginning each morning in the previous day's final
failure
A broken coda, rent life in debris
Basking in echoes off crumbling concrete
Each bounce a lessening
Carried off on time and by distance
Leaving trails on all sides
Yawning off to distant curvatures
And Now is defined by Absence
And Then is a different river
& with each passing second, it's renamed

IV.

Even when it's bad pizza
Music is capable of magic

V.

Books sing songs of their own
Sometimes choral, sometimes guttural
I hum their melodies as I race across this serpent's spine
Feeling the thunder of The Ouroboros we ride
Tearing day into night as it curls into itself

Prayer: flat, rust-flecked harmonies
Under the Great Singing Saw
Wrenching jerks and sways
Flakes flutter in the friction of hands
Buoyed with the stamping of feet

You can dance to damn near anything
I've seen 'em dance for less
Let's call this one "The Can't-Fucking-Get-It-Right
Rag"
It's a new recording of an old song

This is me trying
                              again

I've known edges & there I danced
Never quite achieving abandon
The movements jerky, the muscles ragged, tangled knots
The blade slicing with each of my awkward two-steps
My feet marked out like yearbook eyes
Places where angels wouldn't dare dance

The only thing keeping me from losing the beat
The snare snap of booksong
A chorus of character, the plot a sustained refrain
A new move with each turned page

Trying my best to keep my head up
I doggy-paddle away from the cacophonous maelstroms
of everyday life
Until my feet find purchase in the sucking muck along
the shoreline
And I wade through inky lexicon
Shuffling inch by inch away from the dropoff
Dancing so softly it looks like I'm standing still

**Elegy for J & J**

May you rest easy
With sunlight
Kissing the backs
Of your hands

Celestial fingers
Need no fretboard callouses
The strings ring
Reverberating echoes stretching
            back over themselves
Pulled close like a cloak
Turning inward while hurdling out

A new pinprick luminescence
In the quilted purpled dawn

May you rest easy
Weightless & free

                 ✳

You told us it was all crazy
The sun was so far away
But it could still burn you
& everyone laughed
But you didn't
No, you lived that

May you rest easy
Knowing the sun
*Is* so far away
But it can't burn *you*

＊

It's all dying, the living
Chock full of it, the dying

At first: in parts
Tiny pieces, so minuscule
They're not initially missed
But silt stacks
& we're softer than clay
        Even the hardest of us

Then it's hell & haymakers
A flashflood of it, the living
Right there in the rising waters
Eating with it, working in it
Carrying it to bed
        whenever sleep can be stolen
Waking with it
Higher up the walls than ever before

May you rest easy
Drowning no more

May you rest easy
Beyond making amends

May you rest easy
A surety achieved

May you rest easy
Beyond need
Beyond desire
Beyond degradation
        Remorse

Shame
Beyond that
        pale
        grinning
        sanguine king:
        Suffering

*

May you rest easy
With wildflowers
Behind your ears

May you rest easy
Surrounded by beauty
Smelling of milkweed,
            tobacco, & coffee

May you rest easy
With a harmonica in the key of C
        free of debris & ready
        for the bending of reeds
The mic right there in front of you
Waiting for folly or grace

May you rest easy
Lovingly weeding
The garden of your dreams
Awash in birdsong

May you rest easy
Whistling along the Ottawa
Skipping songs like stones
        across the muddy Maumee
Leaving petals for others to pick

## Running Sound Interference

See this poem is specific
You have to know what faders are
How they're used, what it feels like
To ease them forward, gliding with swells

Swells in volume. I can't just mute the tracks
Of myself that I don't like, that don't fit,
That are beautiful but not right for this session,
This life, this season, this day,

In the DAW I cut and mute, stack and overlap
Focus on dynamics and feel and energy
In life I stumble around dumbfounded
Either on mute or clipping

Accompanying myself on a failed solo

See this is a specific poem
There are bits of me clipping
The lights blinking yellow at first
Then blipping into red & staying there

And I can't remedy the feedback
Can't squelch the piercing wail
With sterilizing compression
Can't back off the mids or the highs

Lord knows I'm beholden to these lows

& there seems to be nothing gained
From easing back on the gain

I want to tell you I'm drowning

Just with dignity and in a minor key

See? This poem is specific
But I think we all know
The last resort
For squelching the feedback
is pulling the plug.

## Even a Little Shit Can Make a Big Stink

Speak straight, walk crooked,
lie if you have to
but make sure it's the whole truth
& nothing but the truth
so help you god,
or whatever doesn't offend you
but still holds you accountable
for the selfish, shameless acts
of isolation, desperation and art
you conjure up and carry out
after a six-pack and a few hits
(or worse, teetotal).

Carry yourself erect
despite your doggedness,
it's the most fluent, constant middle finger
you can raise to gravity and its minions.
I know you're tired, I am too.
Shit, even existence burns calories
and energy doesn't just grow, blossom and fall
like golden and auburn leaves off burdened
existential or cosmological trees.

So make something, any-damn-thing.
Take it from here, there and everywhere in between.
Steal indiscriminately and make it yours.
Slap it together as best you can.
Don't worry about where it came from
or where you think it's going.

If you must, think of it
as the maggots in their wounds.
*Them.* Yes, them. The others,

the can't-make-can't-do-can-only-shit-on-you's.
The ones not capable of turning on their own lights
so they scrape up the backs of gentle giants,
passive savants and you.

The backbiters and bottom feeders,
carrion scavenging on what they could never do,
sure do love to talk and complicate
what's already laid plain,
easy as you go; I'm simple simonizing
the creative sermon, the battle hymn
of the ever-creating republic
and they still can't get it.

So, be the bonfire. Be the flat tire.
Be the cat howling in the night,
the creaking screen door that never would shut right.
Be the infuriating squeak in just their left shoe.

Be the damn after every god,
the crack of the whip,
the rainless clouds covering up the midday sun;
Christ, be the laughing cardboard cylinder
after the last of the toilet paper's gone
because even a little shit
can make a big stink.

## Windsong

I.

Horse-toothed pianos
Pound out pitch keyed laughter

    Beautiful noise
    from tired hands
    & hitch-glitching memory

It slips through the sentinel cattails
    & cartwheels
    across the summer
    stillness of this,
    our nameless pond

It rests amongst the sagging slumber
    of the weeping willow saplings

It settles amongst the overbank
    deposits of last year's
    record setting floods

It nestles down amongst the thistledown
    & coiled brambles
    of this mind's
    gopher-mined
    weed-filled garden

II.

Lightening in the sun
Flash fried white

Yet another birth in reverse
This ouroboros' emesis in aeternum

What's the point of buying the ticket
        when you're already on the ride?

III.

But your songs…
Even when they weren't yours
        they were

You made it so
        Put down your stamp
                with a stomp
        Breathed out your melody
                & sealed it with spit

& if I'm being honest
        I preferred hearing them
                from the other room
        Catching inspiration
                through muted specifics

I, the selfish cyclone
        taking in
        & flinging out
        Inexorably churning

        An unsteady peace
        —An e(I)y(I)e—
                with ever-
                shifting
                boundaries
                somewhere

near the center
Moves like a planchette
—Creative archeology
& messages from
the expanding static
& nobody's ever really sure
if its them
or if it's THEM
but the thing screams
Cap Locks grating
from the grave
& the goosebumps sing
out as they chase
the missives up
slumped spine to coil
behind shining
red rimmed eyes
that waver like
heat shimmers on
late August asphalt

Shifting scrapes filled with windswept debris
Etch in, crosshatched swirling oblivion
Impressionistic renditions
of varying veracity
—is nothing wholly original?
but always scratched
with the ferocity of
desperate love's dying nails
across our collective
windswept sandstone
arch heart


IV.


Hear the windsong

Grains hissing
in the crinkling leaves
like hundreds
of dusty needles
Swelling moan
reverberations
stretch the sound
end over end
before folding it like dough
in a saturated sustain

Slip into chorus
     Love the grit in yer e(I)y(I)e
     Its caress the blinking lid
     Deepening the gashes
     Entering like a splinter
     Lodging like a barb

Windsong plucked you up
     & swept you along
     & it wasn't long before
     you carried the tune
     like a wet paper bag
     holding your last meal

Windsong flowed from you
     —e(I)y(I)e was there—
     Its pulse the bouncing backbeat
     that shook flakes from my friable skull
     & the sandstone arch in my chest
          sent a spray of grains & blood
          steaming up into the purpled night
     The erosion a welcomed alleviation
          A little less of a burden
               for bruised shoulders

A little more space
          between beats
          to suck in quick wisps
          of shuddery breaths

If you survive April's deluge,
          elongate like a reaching petiole,
          or have a radio doused
          with just the right amount
          of susurrated static snow
& if you close your frantic eyes,
          turn your palsied face
          to the fading sun
You might just open like a peony
          & exhale your
          fragrant harmony
          to the windswept
          bouquet

72   *songs for leaving*

A.S. Coomer writes.

Books include *MEMORABILIA, THE FETISHISTS, BIRTH OF A MONSTER, THE DEVIL'S GOSPEL, SHINING THE LIGHT, THE FLOCK UNSEEN, MISDEEDS, FLIRTING WITH DISASTER*, & several others.

Recordings include RURAL EMINENCE VOLUMES I, II, & III, LATE NIGHTS IN PHILPOT, OLD FORT SESSIONS, GODDAMN IT ANYWAY, & several others.

@ascoomer

www.ascoomer.com

# Acknowledgements

Some of the poems included in this collection were previously published in the following publications. Gutter Snob Books wishes to acknowledge them for their fine work and dedication to the small press.

*Can We Have Our Ball Back?*
*Drunk Monkeys*
*pioneertown*
*Rye Whiskey Review*
*Seppuku Quarterly*
*Topical Poetry*

# MORE GUTTER SNOB BOOKS

*SpaceTime Continuum for Dummies*
Michele McDannold

*Noise: art and words*
Misti Rainwater-Lites

*Marilyn: Self-Portrait, Oil on Canvas*
Kerry Trautman

*Running Red Lights*
Aleathia Drehmer

*Texaz Bluez*
Catfish McDaris

*Satan's Kiss*
Alan Catlin

*Proper Etiquette in the Slaughterhouse Line*
James H. Duncan

*As Meaningful As Any Other*
Donna Snyder

*easy and clear*
Jeremy Hight

*Dear So and So*
Rusty Barnes

*Finding Jesus & Prayers to My Saints*
Dan Denton

Made in the USA
Columbia, SC
06 October 2023

24024505R00052